DUMPED

A girl's guide to happiness after heartbreak

Erin Elisabeth Conley

First published in 2007 by
Zest Books, an imprint of Orange Avenue Publishing
35 Stillman Street, Suite 121, San Francisco, CA 94107
www.zestbooks.net

Created and produced by Zest Books, San Francisco, CA
© 2007 by Orange Avenue Publishing LLC
Illustrations © 2007 by Kristin Bowler

Text set in Mrs. Eaves; title and accent text set in Coventry.

Library of Congress Control Number: 2006934912
ISBN-13: 978-0-9772660-1-2
ISBN-10: 0-9772660-1-X

CREDITS
EDITORIAL DIRECTOR: Karen Macklin
CREATIVE DIRECTOR: Hallie Warshaw
WRITER: Erin Elisabeth Conley
EDITOR: Karen Macklin
ILLUSTRATOR: Kristin Bowler
GRAPHIC DESIGNER: Cari McLaughlin
PRODUCTION ARTIST: Cari McLaughlin

Distributed by Publishers Group West

Printed in China.
First printing, 2007
10 9 8 7 6 5 4 3 2 1

Every effort has been made to ensure that the information presented is accurate. Readers are strongly advised to read product labels, follow manufacturers' instructions, and heed warnings. The publisher disclaims any liability for injuries, losses, untoward results, or any other damages that may result from the use of the information in this book.

DUMPED

In the understatement of the century, getting dumped sucks. There's no denying it. And there's nothing worse than that initial moment of truth—the one in which you realize you've gone from loved to left behind. One day you and your beau are sweethearts, ♡ holding hands, strolling down the street. The next day—boom—he's gone, and your universe has evaporated. But, hey, there are worse things, right? Like, um, getting eaten alive by a pack of rabid hamsters or sitting bare-bottomed on a giant nest of wasps. Unfortunately, when you're nursing a broken heart, even these consolations are cold comfort.

So, just how do you cope with the "I'd rather be friends" line? How exactly do you handle unhappily ever after? That's where this Girl's Guide can help. Because even though getting chucked is no fun at all, getting over it actually can be.

You'll be schooled on the potential pitfalls of payback, taught how to throw a pity party, and shown the best way to craft a "Dear Creep" letter. You'll write some bad-breakup haiku and reflect on what you've lost (and, more important, what you have to gain). You'll rely on friends and learn to focus on *you*.

And guess what? Heartbreak is completely unfair and totally democratic: It happens to *everyone*, not just you. Too bad that doesn't make it hurt any less. Still, one thing is certain: You will survive and, eventually, move on to much happier places, at which point you'll wonder why you wasted so much time worrying about him anyway.

Until then, take a nice deep breath and brace yourself.

TABLE OF CONTENTS

1. The Dreaded D-Day: Now What? ... 11

2. Tough Times: Weeping, Wallowing, Wondering

The Dreaded D-Day:
Now What?

First Things First

The day you dreaded has finally come and gone—just like your love life. Your mind is spinning, and your heart hurts. You feel weak in the knees but not in a good way. You may even still be too shocked to see straight. So, what now?

Don't:

- Call your ex. (Wait at *least* a few days or weeks. You don't want to seem desperate.)

- Call his friends. (See above.)

- Make any major decisions or changes in your life. Again, time is your friend here.

Do:

- Inhale, exhale. And then do it again. Some soothing deep breaths will help you stay cool. There'll be plenty of time to react, plot, scheme, worry, and wonder later.

- Call your closest friends and tell trusted family members what's happened. A strong support network is critical to surviving a breakup.

- Let yourself feel what you feel. Fall apart if you need to—just make sure you have something soft to land on.

- Read on …

Missed Signals

Wouldn't it be nice if there were actual signs (in screaming yellow and black) that you could look for when it comes to love? Like PROCEED WITH CAUTION, ROADBLOCK, or DEAD END?

Sure, in retrospect, those early warnings might seem kind of clear. But when you're truly smitten, it can be surprisingly easy to ignore the obvious. For next time, here are a few indications that spell t-r-o-u-b-l-e ahead.

He picked fights about really stupid things, like how much ketchup to slather on your veggie burger.

You hardly ever held hands or kissed anymore, especially in public.

You always seemed to be the one calling, texting, and emailing.

He suddenly got too busy to hang out after school or on the weekends.

He mocked you in front of his friends.

Little things that he used to find adorable—like how you say the word "cute" too much, or your silly laugh—began to annoy him.

He started introducing you to people as his "friend."

He ignored you in the hall or stopped sharing his lunch.

He kept saying, "We need to talk." You kept changing the subject.

He took your picture out of his wallet.

He changed his phone number.

He ran when he saw you.

He started dating one of your friends.

PSST! real-life quotes from real teens

SIGNS THAT THE END IS NEAR

❝When you don't talk at least once a day.
When you don't hug or kiss or anything.
When you can't stand him.❞—14

Love 'Em and Leave 'Em

It may be too late this time around, but why not start wising up for the future while the wound is still fresh? Next time, don't let the butterflies and fireworks fool you. Do a gut check early on. If you get even the faintest whiff of player, freak, or loser, cut 'em loose—pronto! There's no use wasting time with *Mr. Almost*, when you could be entertaining *Mr. Awesome*. It can be tough to tell a guy's flaws when you first meet him, but there are definitely troublesome types to be looking out for.

The Perpetual Player: Of course the bad boy image is hot, but do you really want to be wondering if he's swapping spit with someone else when you aren't around?

The Pill Popper: We all have vices, but watch for excessive or addictive behaviors—like smoking, drinking, cheating, partying, and other potentially destructive habits.

The Fickle Pickle: This boy knows nothing of loyalty and will hightail it the second something "better" comes along. Don't let your heart be a casualty of fussy fellows like these.

The Takes-a-Backseat Boy: We are all guilty of being indecisive from time to time, but do you really want a permanent position in the driver's seat? It's nice to have some power in the relationship, but sometimes it's also nice to sit back, relax, and enjoy the ride.

The Commitment-Phobe: He says yes, yes, yes, when he really means no, no, no. This boy is an expert at making all the right moves, but he stumbles when it comes to being part of a real couple.

The Too-Nice Boy: Nice boys are good, and they don't get enough positive press. But it's the googly-eyed, *too* nice boys that you have to watch out for, with their mama's boy tendencies and lack of backbone. Also known as The Pushover or Cling-On.

The Not So Good, the Bad, and the Ugly

Remember what Thumper's mom said in *Bambi* about not saying anything at all unless it's something nice? Well, if you do remember this saying, try for a moment to forget it. You've just been crushed. And whether you like it or not (not!), you're probably going to spend a lot of time thinking about your ex. So why not think about him in a bad way that just might be good for you?

Take off those rose-colored glasses and try to remember all the irritating, lame, and selfish things about him. You know, the stuff that you overlooked or were hoping to change—like how he rolled his eyes at you all the time or never left a message when he called. Once you get the first few down, it'll be surprisingly easy. In fact, you might want to have an extra sheet of paper nearby.

Six Reasons My Ex Is a Clown:

1. _____

2. _____

3. _____

4. _____

5. _____

6. _____

Forget-Me-Nots: 10 Things to Remember Right After a Breakup

While you are in mourning, you may start to forget things. Simple things. Like brushing your teeth. Here's a list of basics to focus on during the first few days after the end.

1. Breathe. Repeatedly.

2. Sleep. Try it, you might like it.

3. Eat. Preferably something that doesn't come in a can or bag.

4. Be safe. Look both ways before you cross the street.

5. Shower. Or, at the very least, put on a little deodorant—especially if you're going out in public.

6. Think only about the present. Avoid thinking about the past or the future. It'll only make you crazy.

7. Surround yourself with friends and family—the people who love you.

8. Be gentle and forgiving with yourself. You'll probably do a few kooky things, and that's OK—it's normal.

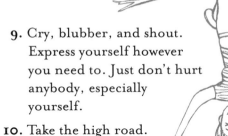

9. Cry, blubber, and shout. Express yourself however you need to. Just don't hurt anybody, especially yourself.

10. Take the high road. Don't gossip or act mean in return, even if you want to. In the end, there's only one person you have to live with forever and you know who that is.

MOVIN' ON

❝Yes, everyone has breakups and eventually everyone gets over it. But the best advice I can give you is that when you're this young, it's not worth worrying about. Overall I think having a relationship is wonderful, but when it ends don't freak out—just move on.❞—15

21

Forget-About-Its:
10 Things Not to Worry About Right After a Breakup

Don't worry—all the agonizing, fretting, and obsessing you're doing is only temporary. And now that you know the most important things to remember during the first few days after your breakup, here's a rundown of what you should overlook:

1. What other people think—especially your ex.

2. Making sense of what went wrong.

3. Trying to pretend like you don't care.

4. How you will ever love—or be loved by— someone else.

5. Boring your friends with the same old sad story again and again. And again.

6. The mountain of tissues piling up by your bed.

7. What to do with the all the little gifts he gave you.

8. Your bruised ego ... and chapped nose.

9. Eating too much chocolate (such as pudding, ice cream, or oversized Kisses).

10. Talking about—or even to—yourself more than usual.

A TOUGH BREAK

❝ I've never been dumped. In fact, I've never actually been asked out. This is a really painful subject and I don't like talking about it. ❞ —14

Lethal One-Liners

No matter how awful it was when your ex delivered the bad news, it probably could have been even worse. Still, if you happen to have heard anything like the lines listed below, consider yourself lucky: You've escaped the harshest human being on the planet.

- Sorry, but you've been replaced by another, more qualified applicant.
- I like you, but my friends don't.
- I really need some space (without you in it).
- I have very low standards, but you don't quite meet them.
- See ya, wouldn't wanna be ya!
- I'm too busy reading the phone book to go out with you again.
- Let's give this another shot in our next lives.

My therapist said I'd be crazy to go out with you.

Better get a Band-Aid 'cause you've just been cut.

real-life quotes from real teens

YOU'RE FIRED

❝I like to think of the world of dating much like the world of business. When I ask someone out it's, 'Welcome on board! I expect to see you in the office on Monday. Bright and early!' So when I dump said person, it's handing them the old pink slip, laying them off.❞ —15

So See-Through

Most people know a backhanded compliment when they hear it. For instance: "Wow, you look better in a bikini than I thought you would." But when it comes to getting dumped, the difference between genuinely thoughtful and quietly crappy can be hard to distinguish. Lame lines to listen out for include:

✗ I think you're really super *sweet* and all, but ...

✗ I know I'll be sorry someday, but ...

✗ It's not you, it's me.

✗ I really need to focus on my [*personal hygiene/ knowledge of UFOs /fill in the lame blank here*].

✗ It's been fun, but I've got to spread the l-u-v.

✗ You're too good for me.

✗ You deserve better.

✗ I'd really like to stay friends.

✗ Thanks, you've really taught me *a lot*.

✗ I'd like to make you happy, but I don't think that's possible.

✗ Somebody (else) is going to be lucky to have you!

✗ This is gonna hurt me more than it's gonna hurt you.

✗ My life is simply too complicated right now.

✗ After seeing me with you, my ex decided we should give it another shot.

✗ You'd be perfect for me, if I wasn't so superficial.

In Other Words ... You've Been Dumped

It doesn't matter what you call it—there's no nice way to say "dumped." But if you feel the need to give your pain a name, there are plenty of ways to phrase it. Take your pick.

abandoned

banished

battle-axed

benched

booted

bumped

burned

cast (away, off, aside)

chucked

Ctrl + Z'd

ding-dong ditched

discarded

ex-changed

ex-terminated

ex-pelled

ex-filed
flushed
given the hurt
heave-hoed
· · · · · · · · · · *jettisoned* · · · ·
kicked to the curb
Little Orphan Annie'd
pink-slipped
put out to pasture
roach moteled
sad sacked
sent packing
set adrift
shucked
slammed
sling shot
· · · · · · · · **smoked**
steam-rolled
tossed (aside, off)
traded in
trashed
Tupper where-d?
unhappily ever aftered
voted off

Terrible Timing:
Top 10 Mortifying Dump Moments

When it comes to being tossed, timing is just one of the factors that can make things feel especially funky. You have every right to buy yourself some extra-expensive tissues—the kind that come in the pretty box—if your *un*beloved cut the cord ...

1. ... just as he casually wrapped his arm around another girl.

2. ... at the homecoming dance, to which you wore the dress you spent three weeks, two days, and five hours picking out in hopes of impressing him.

3. ... the same day your best friend finally hooked up with his best friend—and she can't stop talking about it.

4. ... right after his mom whispered to his dad (loud enough for you to hear), "Well, *that's* not going to last."

5. ... in a lame phone call, starting with lots of ums and followed by, "I don't think I really like girls anymore."

6. ... moments before you got a chance to dump him.

7. ... when everyone at school knew it was coming before you did.

8. ... the day you decided you were madly in love with him.

9. ... the morning after he scored two front-row tickets to see [*fill in the name of your favorite band here*].

10. ... right after you introduced him to your parents, and they loooooooovvvved him.

Tough Times: Weeping, Wallowing, Wondering

How to Feel,
What to Expect

Beneath the whirlwind and warm fuzzies of your
(now lost) l-u-v, the fear of being dumped may have
lurked in your heart—or the thought at least crossed
your mind. But you just weren't *expecting* it. And even if
you actually kind of were, it was probably still a shock.

So once reality sets in, how should you feel? Bummed?
Hurt? Mad? Embarrassed? It's a pointless question. You
will feel however you feel—no matter what any book or
friend or expert tells you. No doubt, you will feel bad.
But you will feel lots of other things, too. That's the
confusing part. Your own emotions may continue to
surprise you. Some days you might feel lucky—like you're
a big-hearted little bird who's escaped a tiny cage. Other
days, you'll feel like you could cry enough tears to fill an
entire bath tub. Or maybe you'll get scared that no one
will ever slide his hand into your back pocket the way your
ex did. You might even find yourself feeling sorry for *him*.
Why? Because, when it comes to love and heartbreak,

anything is possible. That's the beauty and the ugly of it. That, fortunately and unfortunately, is life. Wait out whatever comes … and goes. Whatever it is, there's sure to be more of it.

PSST! real-life quotes from real teens

DWELL IN IT

❝After a breakup, I live in a cave until I feel better about it.❞ —18

Oh Good, Grief!

Obviously, a big split is painful—especially when it wasn't your choice. It can make you feel like you've just lost your best friend, and in some cases that may very likely be true. It's normal to feel sad about what was, what wasn't, and even what might have been. Grieving sounds like a drag, but there's really no getting around it. It's a normal and necessary part of the healing process. According to a famous doctor named Elisabeth Kubler-Ross, there are usually five stages to pass through before you come out singing on the other side.

1. **Denial** ("Did he say *break* up or *make* up?")

2. **Anger** ("I wouldn't take that little sewer rat back if you paid me!")

3. **Bargaining** ("Maybe if I give up gossiping, he'll want me back.")

4. **Depression** ("I need a nap. And a pint of mint chocolate chip ice cream to cry into.")

5. **Acceptance** ("I learned from that relationship and think I'm ready for a new and even better one!")

Of course, not everyone goes through these in order, and sometimes people go through the same stage more than once. Healing is a very personal process. Be patient with yourself.

Cry Me a River

In the land of the dumped, it's healthy—and helpful—to have a good cry. Usually, this requires little assistance, but on the off chance you've already reached your monthly cry quota (or haven't shed a tear since the day you were born), your ducts may need a little nudge. If so, grab some tissues and try these tips to help trigger those tears.

- Think of something really sad. Like a dog with three legs or your pet goldfish floating at the top of the tank.

- Watch *E.T.*, *Bambi,* or a cheesy made-for-TV movie. Eat burnt popcorn.

- Listen to sappy love songs. Think of long-lost exes.

- Spill something permanent on your favorite shirt.

- Stub your toe.

- Overdose on extra-spicy hot sauce.

- Look through old photos of you and your ex.

- Pinch yourself. Hard.

- Express how you truly feel to someone who cares and will listen.

- If all else fails, peel an onion.

GETTING DUMPED STINKS

"Teenagers dump each other every other day. Many don't realize that dumping is a serious issue. It really hurts to lose someone you love.**"**—14

Release: 20 Movies to Curl Up and Cry With

1. *The Sisterhood of the Traveling Pants* (2005)

2. *The Notebook* (2004)

3. *Big Fish* (2003)

4. *Love Actually* (2003)

5. *A Walk to Remember* (2002)

6. *Life as a House* (2001)

7. *Moulin Rouge* (2001)

8. *My Dog Skip* (2000)

9. *Titanic* (1997)

10. *William Shakespeare's Romeo + Juliet* (1996)

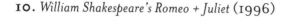

11. *Man in the Moon* (1991)

12. *Edward Scissorhands* (1990)

13. *Ghost* (1990)

14. *Cinema Paradiso* (1989)

15. *Gorillas in the Mist* (1988)

16. *Tonari no Totoro/My Neighbor Totoro* (1988)

17. *Stand By Me* (1986)

18. *E.T., the Extra Terrestrial* (1982)

19. *Kramer vs. Kramer* (1979)

20. *The Way We Were* (1973)

FAIL-SAFE DISTRACTIONS

❝Spend time with your girlfriends, listen to booming music, and eat all the ice cream you can possibly ingest.❞—14

Ruminating

Ruminating is basically a dressed-up word for thinking about something over and over ... and over again. (It also describes how a cow spits up partially digested food and chews it again—gross.) Of course, when you're going through a breakup, it's natural to want to reflect on the past and analyze what went wrong. You might find yourself replaying certain moments (or conversations) between you and your ex. Part of the reason we ruminate is to try to make sense of what's happened. Thinking and talking about your feelings is a good thing, but letting your thoughts spiral out of control can stir up more questions than answers and even lead to serious depression.

But don't despair ... no matter how downhearted you feel, you *can* practice healthy thinking and cut the loop in your brain. All it takes is effort and discipline. Don't expect to magically snap out of it on your first try—your head may have a mind of its own. But with a little patience and some practice, you'll master the art of mind over matter.

Six Steps to Stop Thinking About What's-His-Name:

1. When you notice your mind drifting to the same old place, picture something soothing (palm tree-lined beach, babbling brook, or Grandma's garden) instead.

2. Stop, look, and stare at anything in your line of vision. Pick something and study it carefully. Ask yourself 10 questions about it. (Just don't pick your ex!)

3. Wear a colorful ribbon, string, or rubber band around your wrist (not *too* tight), and give it a little tug each time you notice yourself ruminating.

4. Pick a specific place to let your thoughts about your ex run wild. (But not your bed or any other spot where you hang out or want to feel cozy.) Practice thinking about him there—and not anywhere else.

5. Choose a set window of time each day to think about your ex. When time is up (no more than 15 or 20 minutes max), stop thinking about him and go *do* something instead! Knock a few minutes off your allotted time each day until you're down to zero.

6. Write your thoughts down in a journal or diary. Start with a totally fresh page each day. After a couple of days, try to write at least one positive thought for every negative one.

And, of course, if you find yourself consumed and overwhelmed by repetitive thoughts, or unable to sleep because of them, be sure to talk to a family member about getting professional help.

Indulgences for the Nice and the Naughty

When your heart's been shattered into a million little pieces, there's not much anyone can say or do to patch it right back up again. Talking to friends, moping around the house in your pj's, and imagining a miserable future for your ex *can* ease the pain, but not erase it completely. The good news is that you now have a valid emotional-state license to indulge your every whim, want, wish, and whimper. Take advantage of this amazing, limited-time offer while you can! (Unfortunately, even your dear old Granny's patience will soon wear thin, so mind how long you drag it out.)

Keep in mind that even with the most tragic breakup cases (dumped by smoke signals or via text-message), there's a line between positively pampering and pessimistically poisoning yourself.

Do try these delightful indulgences:

- Painting your toenails an eye-popping pink or outrageous orange.

- Making yourself the guest of honor at your very own spa party for you and five friends.

- Blowing your monthly allowance on those adorable new flats you've been eyeing for months.

- Asking your mom for a foot massage.

- Eating peanut butter chocolate chip cookies in bed.

- Taking a nice long Saturday afternoon nap.

- Skipping one—or *maybe* even two—piano, ballet, or soccer practices.

- Wearing pigtails five days in a row.

- Bringing your beloved childhood stuffed animal to school. (Well-hidden in your backpack, of course.)

- Having veggie pizza for breakfast and cereal for dinner.

- Taking an extra long bubble bath.

- Spending a whole day doing absolutely nothing. And another one staring at the clouds, wishing you were little, stepping on the cracks and picking yourself some flowers.

Don't try these deadly indulges:

- Dying your hair blue or making any other impulsive, *permanent* change to your physical appearance.

- Becoming a total shut-in and refusing to see anyone or go anywhere.

- Blowing your college savings on a revenge billboard to advertise what a chump your ex is.

- Being rude, thankless, and demanding to the people who love you.

- Eating so much cotton candy that your stomach needs to be pumped.

- Hibernating like a big brown bear and sleeping through an entire semester.

- Ditching school, failing tests, quitting piano, ballet, or soccer altogether.

- Wearing the same pair of socks and underwear for days on end.

- Pushing peanuts up your nose—or other bizarre ploys for attention.

- Refusing to eat.

- Using your father's cologne rather than bothering to bathe.

- Doing nothing—after a whole week of doing nothing—to even *try* to make yourself feel better.

- Doing anything illegal or dangerous, and neglecting to ask for help when you really need it.

Moping Essentials:

sappy music

chocolate

girlfriends

box of tissues

pajamas ⋯>

pet

weepy films

old teddy bear

⋯ ice cream

silly magazine

blanket

49

Play 'Em and Weep:
20 Songs to Sigh Over

1. "Bad Day"—Daniel Powter
2. "Maps"—Yeah Yeah Yeahs
3. "Silent Sigh"—Badly Drawn Boy
4. "Let It Be"—The Beatles
5. "Lost Cause"—Beck
6. "Heartbeats"—José González
7. "Hide and Seek"—Imogen Heap
8. "Nothing Compares to You"—Sinead O'Connor
9. "Wake Me Up When September Comes"—Green Day
10. "Slave to Love"—Bryan Ferry
11. "Lonely Day"—Phantom Planet
12. "You Can't Always Get What You Want"—The Rolling Stones
13. "Ring of Fire"—Johnny Cash and June Carter

14. "Forever Young"—Alphaville (or Youth Group)
15. "How to Survive a Broken Heart"—Ben Lee
16. "Hung Up"—Madonna
17. "Beautiful"—Christina Aguilera
18. "Who Knew?"—P!nk
19. "Unpretty"—TLC
20. "Let Go"—Frou Frou

Pity Parties

You're down in the dumps and dateless
on a Friday night. Time to throw yourself a
fabulous pity party! It certainly can't hurt
(unless no one shows), and it might even be
fun. Misery (that would be you) loves company, so
be sure to invite at least a few close friends who are
willing to celebrate the blues and help you laugh, with
you, at yourself.

Suggested Menu: Discomforting Mix of Comfort Foods

Hors d'oeuvres: tortilla chips, fried cheese sticks, pigs
(aka boys) in a blanket

Starters: iceberg salad (dressed with ranch), or creamy
tomato or matzo ball soup

Main dishes: honey-baked ham, boxed mac and cheese,
mashed potatoes

Desserts: warm pie, pints of ice cream, anything
dunkable, crushed Oreos in a glass of milk

Drinks: milkshakes, Dr. Pepper, Shirley Temples, slightly sour lemonade

Suggested Decorations: Pretty ... Pathetic

(Locale: garage, garden shed, or basement)

- balloons that don't float
- cheap neon streamers
- posters of magicians, clowns, or former teen idols
- giant handmade "IT'S MY PARTY AND I'LL CRY IF I WANT TO" sign

Suggested Activities: Games Over

Play "Pin the Tail on the Ex," making sure to use the most unflattering photo you can get your hands on.

Start a mean game of pity poker, betting recklessly with expired bus passes, peanut shells, or dog biscuits.

Make a papier-mâché piñata in your ex's likeness (filled with empty promises rather than candy) and whack away.

Swap most-embarrassing-moments stories.

Laugh, howl, grin, giggle, guffaw—and be glad you're a girl.

Which Is Worse?

Passing gas in front of five of your ex's friends **or** seeing your parents make out?

Doing a face plant in front of your ex's "hot" new girlfriend **OR** going a whole school day with your zipper down?

Being dumped for your best friend *or* swimming in a pool of cactus needles?

Bumping into your ex while wheeling around the block in your Uncle Chester's bright purple electric wheelchair for fun **OR** losing your baby toe in a freak accident?

Hearing your ex telling everyone you have "death breath" **or** having your teeth fall out at age 30?

Having the entire school know you've been dumped before you do *OR* shaving all your hair off?

Being dumped on your birthday **or** getting kicked to the curb on Valentine's?

Seeing your ex kiss someone else **or** eating your brother's smelly socks for breakfast?

Having your ex say he never really liked you that much anyway **OR** never having met your best friend?

Never getting over your first love **or** never even having one?

Hitting Bottom:
How It's Bad, Why It's Good

Everybody has a different bottom. And no, we're not talking about butts, booties, rears, or behinds (even though the same can be said for those as well). For some, hitting bottom might mean there are no more tears left, or that you couldn't stomach your favorite dessert last night. For others, it might mean that your bedroom floor has become lost beneath a mound of clothes and a river of tissues—or that you've started combing your hair with a fork and planning undercover stakeouts in front of your ex's house.

One thing's for certain: Hitting bottom is never pretty. But despite what it seems, it's not just about sinking to a new low. In fact, it could be exactly the kind of kick in the pants you need. After all, when you hit bottom, there's nowhere to go but up.

So, how do you know when you've touched the murkiest depths of down? Oh, you'll know. And slowly, very slowly, you'll start to feel a little more buoyant—a little more like your pre-rejected self. Eventually, you might even start feeling like there's something—or someone—wonderful waiting for you just around the corner. The best part about hitting bottom is just how good it feels again to be back on top.

THE GOOD AND THE BAD

❝It was an addiction. I thought I loved him and that he was the one. He thought otherwise. I dumped him, he dumped me, I dumped him, he dumped me, et cetera. It got old fast.❞—13

Ex-ercise Caution: Avoiding Temptations and Pitfalls

Get Dumped With Dignity

Heartbreak is its own special ailment. There's no diagnosis for it, no magic cure, no easy fix. And its mysterious symptoms might make you feel compelled to do crazy, illogical, outrageous things. Some days you might even look at yourself in the mirror and think, *Huh? Who am I?*

While it may be tough to keep your wits about you, try to think about how you'll feel in the long run. In other words: Don't do anything now that you'll regret later. You don't want to sully your reputation or—more important—compromise your integrity.

Here's the upside: As the dumpee rather than the dumper, you've got the sympathy vote on your side. With a little self-control you can keep it that way, now and *4ever* and always.

- Don't grovel, beg, cry, or plead with him to take you back.

- Don't trash-talk about him with anybody outside your trusted inner circle.

- Be gracious in public. Smile and look as chill as you can, especially if he's around to see you.

- Don't do anything truly nasty or hurtful. And if you do deploy a few innocent revenge tactics, don't get caught.

- Be honest with yourself and those who love you about your feelings.

PSST!
real-life quotes from real teens

TOP THIS

❝A boy left a message on a girl's answering machine saying he hated her and didn't want to see her again. Her parents heard the message first.❞ —14

Bumping Into the Ex

It's bound to happen when—and where—you least expect it: the post-breakup encounter. If you're incredibly lucky, you have just had your hair done and are wearing your übercute new miniskirt. If you're *not* so lucky, you've just come from the dentist and forgotten to take off the bib. Chances are the reality will be somewhere in between.

Tips for playing it cool:

~~▷ You may want to run. Unless you're absolutely sure he hasn't spotted you, don't do it! It will just make you look like a freak.

~~▷ Act cool, but not frigid. Say hey, smile, and move on.

~~▷ Don't stop to chat unless he does. Whatever you manage to say, keep it short and sweet.

~~▷ Don't take this opportunity to put him down. And don't bring up the past. It'll only validate his decision to bail.

≈ Try not to brag excessively or talk about how fabulous your life is now. He'll see right through it.

≈ Rise above it all and be your very best self. And remember, he was lucky to have you!

PSST!
real-life quotes from real teens

THE SHOWDOWN

❝I was with my new man at the movies and ran into the boy I'd been seeing over the summer. I saw him coming and flipped out. I wasn't ready to see him—I wasn't over him—but I had no choice but to keep walking towards him. The boy I was currently with—when he realized who it was—put his arm around me, and we went to face the music. My ex saw me and I swear he smiled because he always had a thing for showdowns. We walked up to him and talked for a couple of minutes, and he lost interest when he couldn't get a rise out of either of us. As we walked away, I went over the many scenarios that could have happened but didn't.❞—15

How to Lose and Keep Your Cool

It's OK to get angry. In fact, it's all part of the process. But there are healthy ways to unleash your wrath. Some of your anger might come from the way you were treated, or it could come simply from the fact that what happened is not what you wanted. He's gone, and it's out of your control. That can be maddening.

To confuse things further, sometimes it can be hard to get peeved at the former object of your affection. And so your frustration might rear its ugly head in unusual, hideous ways (screaming, "I SAID, NO THANKS!" when the guy at the fast-food counter mistakenly asks, "Would you like fries with that?" a second time). Any anger you feel boils down to this: You're hurt and sad.

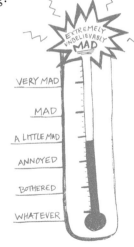

EXTREMELY UNBELIEVABLY MAD

VERY MAD

MAD

A LITTLE MAD

ANNOYED

BOTHERED

WHATEVER

It's simple and complicated, just like love. So let it out ... wisely.

- Rant, rave, yip, scowl, and blow your top somewhere private. Own your anger. Shout "I am MAD at [insert name] and that's OK!" After a while, you'll be too tired to yell anymore—at least until the next time.

- Take up kickboxing, karate, or some other contact sport.

- Do something creative to record your feelings, like writing a diary or blog. (If you feel like going public with it, be sure to wait a few days—or better yet, months—before you do. You may change your mind.)

- Pop bubble wrap, stomp on a cardboard box, throw rocks into a lake, rip an old phonebook to shreds, or crush aluminum cans (recycling them afterward, of course).

PSST!
real-life quotes from real teens

LOSING YOUR COOL

❝Throw him to the wolves. Just kidding. I usually envision him getting humiliated in front of a huge crowd, like toilet paper on his shoe or tripping. Everyone would laugh, and he'd look at me for help, but I'd laugh too. It's great therapy.❞—15

Dialing Is for Dummies

Your phone is probably just sitting there, taunting you: *Call him. What's the harm? It's just talking.* You will feel tempted to make that call. It's practically breakup protocol.

Repeat after me: I will feel tempted, but I will not give in.

Keep your fingers busy with other things. Take up knitting, piano, or finger-puppetry. If you find yourself poised to dial, call a friend instead! Until you're really totally and fully o-v-e-r it, calling will only make you feel worse. He won't answer, or he'll likely be cold and awkward if he does. Even worse, he could be super nice and indulge you, which will just make you fall for him all over again. If he wanted you back, he'd call you—not the other way around. Harsh, yes, but true. Sorry.

HOW TO HANDLE HEARTBREAK

❝First, depending on how much I liked him, I cry. Then I call my best friend, and she comes over before I jump out a window. It is soooooooooo comforting to have her there with me. Then I usually go out and find other boys. It's good to know that you can do better and he really wasn't worth all the sobs.❞—16

It's Payback Time!

OK, so sometimes revenge really is sweet. Here are 10 fiendish—and fantastic—ways to pay back your ex for tossing you aside.

1. Line his toilet seat with clear gel toothpaste.
2. Lace his soft drink (or other beverage) with prune juice.
3. Put itching powder in his shorts.
4. Steal his homework and turn it (anonymously) in late.
5. Write "I ♡ my mom" on his notebook.
6. Stick a big sign on his back that says, "I'M A BED-WETTER."
7. Send five large anchovy pizzas to his house.
8. Hide his favorite possession.
9. Fill his gym socks with gravy.
10. Flirt shamelessly with his arch nemesis.

Pranks aside, don't forget that sometimes the best revenge is just to get on with it, be happy again, and forget he ever existed. Also, before you do anything *too* mean, remember that the old stupid saying— "what goes around, comes around"—is, usually, a true stupid saying.

PSST!

real-life quotes from real teens

SWEET REVENGE

❝I think one of my fantasy punishments would be to see my ex-boyfriend get a new girlfriend, then do something stupid. His new girlfriend would yell at him, break up with him, and pour her drink on his head. This would all be in public. I think I would have a field day with this.❞—15

69

Dear Creep Letter

Did your boyfriend treat you like trash? Did he ignore you in public and embarrass you in front of friends? Whatever lousy way he acted, there are still plenty of chances to take back your power and move on to bigger and better things. One way is to set the record straight with a "so long, sucker" form letter. Go on, pick up that pen and rewrite history the way it should have gone down in the first place!

See the list on pages 72 and 73 to fill in the blanks.

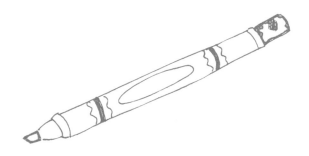

Dear [*fill in name or other choice word here*],

This may come as a bit of a shock to you, but I think you're [*choose from list* **A**], **so I'm going to have to** [*choose from list* **B**]. **I'm sorry for doing this, but** [*choose from list* **C**]. **I know we had some really** [*choose from list* **D**] **times, but it's time for me to** [*choose from list* **E**]. **I'm sure you're** [*choose from list* **F**] **understand. I want you to know that I'll always be** [*choose from list* **G**]. **So take care and good luck with that** [*choose from list* **H**] **problem.**

So long sucker,

[*Fill in your name here*]

A

a total loser
less likable than an angry clown
really irritating

B

kick you to the curb
pretend we never met
turn you into the police

C

it gives me great pleasure
you really do smell
your best friend says I should

D

crappy
wretched
god-awful

E

start dating your brother
floss my teeth
find someone I can stand

F

too much of a tool to
too busy staring in the mirror to
never going to get over me, much less

G

too good for you
the best thing you ever had
delighted I gave you the heave-ho

H

gas
body odor
hair loss

Too Bad, Sucka: 10 Clever Ways to Make Him Regret It

1. Act like you don't care.

2. Laugh heartily with friends whenever he passes by. Act like you have no idea he's in the vicinity.

3. Start going out with his best friend.

4. Paint a fake hickey on your neck. Make sure it looks real!

5. Bring a hot new boy to the local hangout spot. Be noticed by mutual friends. Flirt shamelessly.

6. Become super chums with his older sibling.

7. Have flowers or a cool gift delivered to you in the school cafeteria.

8. Get your friend to let it slip that your new mystery man is an Italian model who's notoriously romantic.

9. Buy a gorgeous, girly new dress for the school dance. Strut your stuff on the floor.

10. Look—and feel—fabulous. Most of all, be happy.

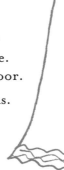

PSST!

real-life quotes from real teens

ANOTHER WAY TO MAKE HIM REGRET IT ...

❝Punch him in the face. Have him go through the same pain I went through.❞ —18

Learning to Deal: Hoping and Coping

Heart Healers and New Mindset Mantras

The breakup wound may still be fresh, but it's never too soon to start spending your energy in a more hopeful and positive place—and, no, that doesn't mean the mall. What it does mean is practicing healthy thinking and setting good intentions for yourself.

Sound a little too hippie-dippy for you? Pocket that judgment and keep reading, Little Rainbow. You might be surprised by how helpful this stuff can be, given the right (and, in this case, desperate) circumstances. Think of the exercises listed below as kind of like spinach for the soul—or happy pills that you don't have to pop. They'll make you stronger faster and feel better right away, even if only for a little bit.

Things you'll need: An open mind, a dash of self-discipline, a pretty blank book, and a colorful pen.

Heart Healers

Gratitude Lists

First thing in the morning, before you let your feet hit the floor, write down five things you are thankful for. Be as specific as possible (think: the smell of your grandmother's perfume, the sound of your best friend's laugh, an A on the math final, your old Hello Kitty socks, cherry blossom trees, bunnies, and bubblegum). Do this five days (or more) in a row and the world will look seriously less sucky.

Pick-Me-Ups

This one's easy: Do something nice for yourself each and every day. You might treat yourself to a big scoop of ice cream, give your hair a deluxe deep-conditioning treatment, or go for a refreshing swim. Keep a record of your daily pamperings. Taking a moment to go back over all those goodies is a pick-me-up in and of itself.

Affirmative Actions

Try doing a random good deed a day for at least a full week. It can be smallish (inviting the new girl to eat with you and your friends, or braiding your little sis's hair so your mom doesn't have to) or biggish (risking your rep to defend the class dork or giving up precious weekend time to serve soup at the local homeless shelter). You'll see that the more good you do, the more good you get. It's one of those magical rules of the universe.

New Mindset Mantras

A mantra is kind of like a spoken wish. The idea (which comes from certain ancient religions) is that if you verbalize your desire it will come to be. Your mantra might actually be something you already know about yourself but seem to have forgotten lately ("I am a beautiful girl, inside and out, and any boy would be lucky to have me," or "I am an awesome soccer player and will help lead my team to victory").

Find a quiet place to sit comfortably. Clear your mind, close your eyes, take some deep breaths, and repeat your chosen mantra—just a few minutes at a time to start. And later, if you find yourself getting glum, you can repeat it (to yourself) again and again if you need to. It's a simple exercise that will help keep your mind focused on the present and the positive.

Some ideas for New Mindset Mantras:

He was lucky to have had me. I was lucky to lose him.

One door closes, another door opens.

Some days you're the fly. Other days you're the windshield.

ONE GIRL'S HEALING HABITS

❝I go shopping, have a manicure, and have a night in with my best friend. We watch videos, talk about girl power, and condemn the male sex. Then, I start working out a lot because I want to look my best the next time I see him (this includes buying a new outfit). I also listen to all the music I liked and he never really dug. Basically, it's a freeing experience.❞ —15

The Five Ws ... and the Rest of the Alphabet, Too

In the days and weeks that follow your bust-up, you may find yourself wandering around, wondering about the Ws of your demise: the who, what, where, why, and when of it all. There are a million variations on these questions, but classics range from **who** *does he think he is*? to **what** *could I have done differently*? to **where** *did things go wrong*? and **why** *doesn't he like me anymore*? And, of course, there's always **when** *will I feel better*?

Dust off your old diary, notebook, or journal (or get a new one), and write your way through the **Ws**. Putting your feelings down on paper is an excellent way to make sense of the jumble in your brain. Once you get the hang of it, things you didn't even know you were thinking will just pop up on the page. Most important, writing will help you heal. Oh, and if you draw a blank, just doodle. Doodles are therapeutic, too.

Light(en Up) Reading:
20 Good Books to Get You Beyond the Boo-Hoos

1. *Emma* by Jane Austen

2. *Girl Goddess #9* by Francesca Lia Block

3. *The Sisterhood of the Traveling Pants* by Ann Brashares

4. *Jane Eyre* by Charlotte Brontë

5. *All-American Girl* by Meg Cabot

6. *My Antonia* by Willa Cather

7. *Truth or Dairy* by Catherine Clark

8. *Gingerbread* by Rachel Cohn

9. *Oh the Places You'll Go* by Dr. Seuss

10. *Prom* by Laurie Halse Anderson

11. *Harold and the Purple Crayon* by Crockett Johnson

12. *To Kill a Mockingbird* by Harper Lee

13. *The Boyfriend List: (15 Guys, 11 Shrink Appointments, 4 Ceramic Frogs and Me, Ruby Oliver)* by E. Lockhart

14. *The Earth, My Butt, and Other Big Round Things* by Carolyn Mackler

15. *Sloppy Firsts: A Novel* by Megan McCafferty

16. *The Year Of Secret Assignments* by Jaclyn Moriarty

17. *ttyl* by Lauren Myracle

18. *Angus, Thongs and Full-Frontal Snogging: Confessions of Georgia Nicolson* by Louise Rennison

19. *The Catcher in the Rye* by J.D. Salinger

20. *The Adrian Mole Diaries* by Sue Townsend

Shouldn't I Be Over This Already?

It is sometimes said that it takes one-third the time you were in a relationship to really, truly get over it. It is also sometimes said that math is easy and brussels sprouts are good. Forget about letting anyone else put an expiration date on your breakup blues. The healing process is totally personal and something that depends on more than just one factor. Who you are, how it ended, your past experiences, the strength of your support network— all these things and more play into how you will respond to the end of your relationship.

And we are often our own harshest critics. Give yourself a break. It might take more (or less) time than you expect before you're ready to jump into your next crush's lap. Don't be discouraged if one day you feel like, Wow, I'm SO over this!, only to be back in the dumps again the next. No matter how far you have to go, there will come a day, in the not-too-distant future, when it will all be like life before the iPod: ancient history.

the Best
Friend Hug

OH, THE PAIN

**It hurts. I keep most of it hidden away until
the hurt goes away and then it's time to laugh again.** —17

Haiku You Do This to Me?

Love—and the loss of it—has inspired some very bad poetry throughout the ages. But if it makes YOU feel better, why not give it a whack? And there's always the possibility you might even have talent.

There are lots of different types of poetic expression to try: free verse, sonnets, limericks, and rap, to name a few. But haiku can be especially beneficial in times of stress. It's an old, beautiful, and breezy Japanese art form. A haiku is kind of like a snapshot that captures the essence of a brief moment in time and the feeling behind it. Each poem consists of just three short lines—with exactly five syllables in the first, seven in the second, and five in the third: **5-7-5**. Simple to remember ... yet not easy to do.

You might find the focus it takes to craft a haiku strangely relaxing.

Sample breakup haiku:

Colored candy hearts
crushed on the sidewalk next to
that old picture: us

The Cute Movie Cure:
25 Flicks to Brighten Your Mood

1. *Nacho Libre* (2006)

2. *Pride and Prejudice* (2005)

3. *13 Going On 30* (2004)

4. *Dodge Ball: A True Underdog Story* (2004)

5. *Mean Girls* (2004)

6. *Napoleon Dynamite* (2004)

7. *Down With Love* (2003)

8. *Elf* (2003)

9. *Finding Nemo* (2003)

10. *Saved!* (2003)

11. *School of Rock* (2003)

12. *What a Girl Wants* (2003)

13. *About a Boy* (2002)

14. *Sweet Home Alabama* (2002)

15. *Legally Blonde* (2001)

16. *The Princess Diaries* (2001) **and** *The Princess Diaries 2: Royal Engagement* (2004)

17. *Shrek* (2001) **and** *Shrek 2* (2004)

18. *Best in Show* (2000)

19. *Bring It On* (2000)

20. *Rushmore* (1999)

21. *The Truth About Cats and Dogs* (1996)

22. *Clueless* (1995)

23. *The Princess Bride* (1987)

24. *Ferris Bueller's Day Off* (1986)

25. *Sixteen Candles* (1984)

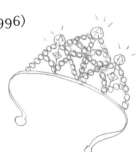

Petty Fours

These little exercises are in honor of all the crummy little things he did. They are little and silly and just 4 fun.

1. Let your four closest friends do their best mean imitation of him.

2. Think of four guys you'd rather go out with than him. (Sky's the limit!)

3. Bake him four chocolate-covered dirt cupcakes and have them delivered to his doorstep.

4. Finally forget he ever existed—at least for the next four minutes.

PSST!
real-life quotes
from real teens

PETTY JERKS

"We live in a small town so we have to take a bus into the next town where the school is. There's this boy from the other town (so nobody really knows him), and it sounds like he's been out with a LOT of girls. He's going back and forth between two of my friends right now. They have both gone out with him already and broken up, but he flirts with both of them and I KNOW he's going to ask one of them out. The rest of the girls in my grade all hate him with a passion, and we try to tell Carrie and Liz, but they won't listen. We just have to sit back, watch him hurt them, and hope they learn their lesson. I will NEVER go out with him. I think he's an immature little brat who looks like a monkey, and my other friends think he looks like a mole!"—13

The Ex-Files

In the name of self-preservation, it's time to ditch the old photos, lose the letters, and chuck the giant, cuddly panda he won for you at the fair. You don't have to start a bonfire or make a trip to the dump (pun intended) with all the lovely little mementos of your days (weeks, months, or years) together, but you do need to put it away—out of sight and mind—for the foreseeable future.

Find a pretty box, and decorate and label it with something nice and simple—something that has meaning to you and your relationship with your ex. Play music (see "Songs to Sigh Over" in Chapter Two) and let yourself feel whatever you feel as you box up the past, tape it shut, and tuck it away. It's OK to be sad because it *is* sad. But it's also time to say good-bye.

PSST!

real-life quotes
from real teens

ADVICE ON EX-FILING

❝You should take his stuff and burn it. That made me feel better. (It also made a cozy fire to sit by.) Listen to a lot of old sad songs and new ones, too. It always makes me feel better to know that others are in pain as well.❞—13

The Bright Side: Getting Up, Getting On, Getting Over It

The Beauty of Being Single: 20 Reasons Why It Ain't So Bad

I'm going to grow up to be one of those little, old, lonely ladies that has no one to love but 29 cats.

If you are newly single, this thought may have crossed your mind. Don't worry—it's a pretty standard fear. Being cut loose from your loved one *is* scary. But, guess what? It can also be quite liberating. Never thought of it that way? Take a look at the following list for a fresh perspective on just how good going solo can be.

1. You don't have to pretend to enjoy what he does.

2. You've got one less birthday gift to buy, which means more moola for you!

3. If there's a little lunch left in your teeth, it's a minor, not a major, tragedy.

4. You can take your stuffed animals back out of the closet.

5. You'll have more free time to bake cupcakes with your cousin, listen to music, study rocket science, or hangout with friends.

6. You don't have to wonder when the ax will fall, since it already has.

7. You don't have to waste time decoding his comments.

8. Or tracking his whereabouts.

9. You don't have to pretend to laugh at his gross and stupid jokes.

10. You can play soccer, volleyball, and video games yourself instead of watching him do it.

11. Now, the popcorn bucket is *all* yours at the movies.

12. You can tell your friends all the truly embarrassing things about him, like how he made that weird clucking noise when he was "thinking."

13. You can imitate his dorky moves.

14. You can wear your hair up as much as you like.

15. You can eat at a leisurely pace, since he's not there to scarf down what you haven't finished yet.

16. You can wear your old sockittens—those knee-highs with the rainbow-colored stripes and individual toes—without judgment.

17. When you go swimming, you can stay in the shallow end doing handstands with your friends, or chicken out on the high dive.

18. You can introduce the hot new foreign exchange student to your local customs.

19. You can stroke your own ego, rather than his.

20. You are now available for your next boyfriend, who is bound to be better.

PSST!

real-life quotes from real teens

SPREAD YOUR WINGS

❝Meet boys from all over the place. Don't focus on just one. Get to know them. Don't dwell on the past, it will only make things worse.❞ —13

Bust a Move

It'd be a lot easier to lick your wounds from the comfort of your couch, watching reality TV with your two old friends—Mr. Bag of Doritos and Ms. Can of Coke—to keep you company. At this point, it may even be hard for your mouth to form the word "ex-er-cise." But "blobbing out"—now that rolls right off the tongue.

Sometimes it's nice to do nada, but eventually, as in NOW, you've got to fight inertia and bust a move. Studies show that exercise helps you release hormones called endorphins, which make you feel happier. In other words, the more you move, the more you'll *want* to move amongst the living again.

And exercise doesn't have to be dead boring or routine. There's more to it than running circles around the track or burning rubber on the treadmill. It can be fun, creative, and social. Who knows how many cute boys are at the dojo, waiting for you to give them a karate chop? Hiiiiiiiiyah!

So, where to start? Anywhere, somewhere … soon. Some suggestions to get you going:

Feel Like a Little Kid Again

Play circus arts, dodgeball, handball, hopscotch, jump rope, or tetherball, or just hop on a trampoline or a swing.

Do Something Different

Learn archery, badminton, fencing, Frisbee, golf, horseback riding, or kayaking.

Ex-Games

Go kitesurfing, kickboxing, mountain biking, surfing, skateboarding, skimboarding, or snowboarding.

Grace Under Pressure

Pick up ballet, hula, ice-skating, or pilates.

Mind, Body, and Soul

Do hip-hop in a group or martial arts with a sensei, power walk with friends, or practice yoga in the studio.

There's No "I" In Team

Cheer for football, play field hockey or soccer, shoot hoops, swim laps, or run around the tennis court.

If you're new to exercising, start slowly. You don't want to add injury to insult (being dumped)! Be sure to stretch before and after, and drink plenty of water. Check with your doctor first if you have any health issues, like asthma or diabetes.

PSST!
real-life quotes
from real teens

SOCCER BALL SORROWS

❝I was dating this boy on my soccer team, and I left my
ball with him and then dumped him before I got it back.
The day after, he brought it to school and gave it to me.
I tried to talk to him because I still wanted to be friends,
but it was so awkward. We were both crying.❞ —13

Get Crafty

Being creative is a promising way to channel your uncheerfulness. Ever hear of the Mexican artist Frida Kahlo? Check out her bio online and you might start to think maybe you aren't SO tortured after all. She turned her misery into masterpieces. And now that you've been ex-filed, you can too. (Hello, silver lining!)

Learning something new will help you forget what's-his-face *and* become a more interesting, well-rounded person. Maybe you already have an inkling of where your talent lies, or maybe you haven't got a clue. Either way, have fun and let your crafty girl go at it.

So many pursuits to pick from — where to start?

Start Acting Up

Set heartbreak aside and become a
real-life drama queen by taking acting lessons or trying
out for the school play. Who knows, maybe you're an Anne
(Hathaway), Keira (Knightly), Scarlett (Johansson), or
[*insert favorite Hollywood golden girl here*] in the making?

Origami Swami

Surprise friends and family with precious little paper gifts
made by hand. Mastering the ancient art of origami is a
truly original pastime that will set you apart from the
run-of-the-papermill crowd. Itty-bitty pink-and-
orange-flowered boats, butterflies, and cranes: What
could be cuter?

Imagine Knit

Unless you've been trapped under a giant crocheted
oven mitt for the past couple of years, you already know
that knitting is not just for little old ladies anymore. You

can craft adorable accessories like lap-dog scarves, cell-phone socks, leg warmers, bikinis, and more. Pick up one of the million books on the market or sign up for class at the local knitting shop. You have time on your hands—now all you need is some pretty yarn, special sticks, and nimble fingers.

Play it Up

Get plucky and take up guitar (or accordion or piano or ukulele or whatever) and evolve from dumped to pumped. There's magic in making music. And a girl musician is way cooler than your generic rocker guy. Gwen, Pink, Fiona, Avril, Alicia—the sooner you start those lessons, the sooner you can add your name to that list.

The Art of Giving

Some say that helping others is an art unto itself. So why not pull yourself up by those pitiful bootstraps and try volunteering at an old folk's home, a children's hospital, or the Humane Society? One of the many pluses of helping others is that it helps you, too. You just may find all the love you feel you're missing now returned to you tenfold.

Pop Quiz!
Are You *Really* Over It?

Feel like you've finally put all that history behind you? Take this handy quiz to find out whether you're stuck on the slow boat to China or speeding past on the *Orient Ex-press*. Be honest and don't worry—no matter how you score, you're bound for an exciting new destination … eventually.

1. You hear that your ex is directing your school's latest production of *The Wizard of Oz*. You:

A. Join the cast in the only remaining role: Toto, Dorothy's faithful canine sidekick.

B. Start rumors about what a total snoozer it's going to be.

C. Wish him well, but make sure you have other exciting plans on opening night.

D. Splurge on a fabulous dress and hire a hot date for the premiere.

2. You bump into your ex in the tampon aisle at the supermarket. You:

A. Hold your breath, turn beet-red, and make a run for it.

B. Sneer and drop a few boxes of adult diapers into his cart when he's not looking.

C. Discreetly place your products under a box of cookies and stop for a brief, friendly chat.

D. Pause, but only to say that your new boyfriend is out front, waiting for you in his convertible.

3. The cute clerk at the new local café asks if you'd like to hang out sometime. You:

A. Say thanks, but you and your ex are still trying to work things out.

B. Tell him that you already have a dog—one that would never lie or cheat.

C. Smile and say, "Yeah, that'd be nice."

D. Agree, and make sure your ex will be there to watch you spoon-feed flan to your date.

4. **Your song—the one that was playing when you two first kissed—comes on the radio in your friend's dad's car. You:**

A. Ask your friend's dad to turn the volume up—all the way up, to 11.

B. Tell your friend's dad to pull over so you can get out and vomit.

C. Remember all those pre-ex times you listened to—and genuinely *liked*—that song.

D. Dial your ex and put your cell up to the speaker.

If you answered mostly As: You are extremely sensitive and loyal. When you fall, it's off a cliff—so it might take you a little longer than others to let go of an ex. Be half as patient with yourself as you were with him, and you'll be fine. Just you wait and see.

If you answered mostly Bs: You still have a lot of anger toward your ex. It's OK to be mad, but make sure you don't become plain old bitter. That's never pretty. Talking to a therapist might help you get to the bottom of your rage and on to the bright future ahead.

If you answered mostly Cs: You may still have a down moment here and there, but your heart seems pretty well-patched. Nicely done! Just be sure to check how deep the water is before diving headfirst into another relationship. And don't forget there's nothing wrong with going solo for a while.

If you answered mostly Ds: You seem to have some lingering, unresolved feelings about your ex. Wanting to make him feel sorry is natural, but it's not exactly healthy. Try to focus on yourself—what you're doing and feeling—rather than him, and you'll be liberated in no time.

Upbeat: 20 Songs of Freedom

1. "Extraordinary Machine"—Fiona Apple

2. "Put Your Records On"—Corinne Bailey Rice

3. "Since You've Been Gone"—Kelly Clarkson

4. "Someday You Will Be Loved"—Death Cab for Cutie

5. "Mushaboom"—Feist

6. "Walk Away"—Franz Ferdinand

7. "I'm Like a Bird"—Nelly Furtado

8. "Feel Good Inc."—Gorillaz

9. "I Believe"—Chris Isaak

10. "Everyday I Love You Less and Less"—Kaiser Chiefs

11. "Welcome Back"—Mase

12. "Float On"—Modest Mouse

13. "Light & Day"—The Polyphonic Spree

14. "Top of the World"—Shonen Knife

15. "The Comeback"—Shout Out Louds

16. "L.O.V.E."—Ashlee Simpson

17. "Hundreds of Sparrows"—Sparklehorse

18. "Cool"—Gwen Stefani

19. "Me Voy"—Julieta Venegas

20. "I Wish You"—Rachel Yamagata

PSST!
real-life quotes from real teens

MUSICAL MEDICINE

❝The one thing that definitely makes me feel better is music. I love hearing that someone has gone through the same thing as me.❞—13

Reasons Why You Rule

Being aware of your strengths is always important—especially in times of weakness (like those days when you feel like a pigeon, looking for sandwich crusts in the gutter). But can you remember the last time you *really* thought about all the good things you have to offer the world? Honestly?

Make a list of eight (or more) great things about yourself. Be as specific as possible. Here are some examples:

1. *I'm an excellent listener.*

2. *I always empty the dishwasher (even when I don't want to) without grumbling.*

3. *I hold my grandfather's hand when we cross the street.*

4. *My nose crinkles up cutely when I laugh.*

Putting these personal props down on paper may feel funny at first. Relax. It doesn't mean you think you're hot s@#t or better than anybody else—just that you can remember the inherent beauty in you.

PSST!

real-life quotes from real teens

GETTING ON WITH IT

❝Just remember you're a great person. Don't let a boy get you down.❞—15

Friends With the Enemy

Six little words you never want to hear: I really want to stay *friends*. It's the ultimate breakup cliché. But at some point, after a bit of time has passed, this issue may become a genuine question. One day you're two peas sharing an iPod, and the next you're forced to act like strangers. It's weird.

So what … stick around long enough to see him start dating someone else? Some people would say that's like pouring Pop Rocks into an open wound. But actually being friends with your ex isn't totally out of the question. People DO do it. Look at Bruce and Demi (and Ashton). OK, they were *married* and have kids but still … it's possible.

But you also need to consider if you can handle being "just buds." And about how much you really liked him as a friend in the first place, before all the cuddling and stuff. If the answers are "no" and "so-so," respectively, invest in other *frelationships* instead.

Either choice—morphing into future friends or staying strictly former flames—won't be easy in the beginning. Take your time. If he was sincere about wanting to keep in *ttyl*-land, he'll wait for you to make contact again when you're ready. Until then, *bbfn* will have to do.

IT'S A FRIEND FLING

" I stalked this one boy for about a year after we broke up. That was interesting. I kept on trying to get back together with him again and he just wouldn't have it. Finally after a year, we both got over it and became friends. But then, about six months after that we got together again.**"** —16

Dump Unto Others

Believe it or not, the day will come when you are in the position of having to dump someone yourself. It may not be as hurtful as having your heart squashed, but it's not entirely cozy either. When that time comes, try to remember how it felt to be on the other side.

And if you ever feel a little fuzzy on good breakup behavior, you can always refer back to this list.

1. Once you know that your heart's no longer in it, don't let it drag out until it's just so painfully obvious that nothing needs to be said anyway.

2. Don't do it over the phone—or by email, IM, text, or pigeon-carrier (aka having your **bff** give him the kiss-off for you). Don't do it any other way but face-to-face, in person.

3. Don't start acting like a fool just so he'll break up with you.

4. Don't start another relationship until you're out of your current one. It's disrespectful to everyone, including yourself.

5. Have patience. Talk *and* listen. Be willing to put in the time and answer all the inevitable "but why?" questions.

6. Be clear and compassionate. Don't point out all the little things that annoyed you, but do try to be as honest as possible.

PSST! real-life quotes from real teens

LIFE LESSONS LEARNED

❝I must admit that without dumping, we wouldn't be ready for what's out there in the real world.❞ —14

Something to Celebrate

So now that you've cried and moped, hoped and healed, it's time to resurface. Someday soon—maybe even (shock!) today—you'll be ready to dip your baby toe back into the dating pool. When you do, try to do it with an open heart and mind. Exercising caution is fine, but don't be so sure you'll be able to see that next cannonball coming before it drops on you.

Tuck away the bitterness of the past—that's where it should be kept. You've come out the other side of something rough and survived—a better, stronger, and more beautiful person. That is something to celebrate!

PSST!
real-life quotes
from real teens

NEW LOVE

❝When my boyfriend broke up with me for the fifth—
and final—time, I was crushed. Getting back to life was
incredibly hard. A few months later, when it seemed like
life would never look up, this sweet hippie at work with
puppy-dog brown eyes started hanging around. Without
even thinking about it, I started hoping he'd come by. And
over the next few weeks it turned into a major crush—on
both sides. All of a sudden I felt happy again, looked for-
ward to getting up in the morning, and felt a major weight
lifted. A new crush was the cure for me—and it's best when
it happens when you aren't even thinking about it.❞—18

Quick Refresher:
10 First Date Tips

Now that those love wounds have healed, you might soon be ready to give Cupid another shot. No matter how long you've been out of play, your romantic instincts—how to flirt and get cozy, date and be wooed—will probably kick right back in automatically. But just in case you're a little rusty, here are a few things to remember for that very next great first date:

1. Keep it short and sweet. Plan a graceful (and legit) escape hatch for an hour or two later.

2. Make it an afternoon outing—something casual like lunch, coffee, or a stroll. Somehow the stakes seem higher post-sundown.

3. Don't start thinking about how cute your kids would be just because he's so good-looking. Gray matter matters!

4. Don't answer the phone on the first ring. And don't call him back immediately. Make him wait (a little) and wonder. A bit of mystery can be a potent aphrodisiac.

5. Don't agree to that second date on the spot. Check your calendar first, even if you don't have one.

6. Don't push for something definite if it's not there. If he doesn't rave about you and what a great time he had, it doesn't necessarily mean anything. Only time can tell, and no one likes the smell of insecurity or desperation.

7. Watch for signs. If he's staring at your lips, he probably wants to kiss you.

8. Leave him wanting more. If he does seem to want a kiss, you might take the opportunity to flash a flirty smile, say thanks, and pop into your house—instead of letting him have one. Yet.

9. If you genuinely had a good time—and you're not completely delusional—relax. He probably did, too. You'll hear about how much fun it was on another date to come.

10. Don't forget that you are a great catch. But that doesn't mean you have to swim circles, waiting to be snatched up. Cast a line and fish for yourself! Just don't forget to rip out the hook and throw the small-minded ones back …

Fly, Be Free!

This is the start of a whole new chapter for you—and the end of this book. Good things are out there, waiting to unfold at your feet. Before you bolt, take a moment to make yourself a few promises. Create a list of plans, dreams, wishes, and goals. Big and small, bright and beautiful—whatever they are, put 'em down for posterity. That way, they are even more likely to come true.

Plans:

_____

_____

_____

Dreams:

_____

_____

_____

Wishes:

_____

_____

_____

Goals:

_____

_____

_____

_____

about the author

Erin Elisabeth Conley is a freelance writer and editor who splits her time between Buenos Aires, Argentina, and San Francisco, California. She brings her bratty cat Mouche with her wherever she goes. She considers herself somewhat of an expert on being dumped, but still feels lucky in love.